AN ALTERNATIVE ORTHODOXY

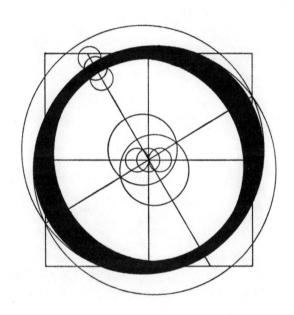

ORDER
DISORDER
REORDER

VOL. 8 NO. 2   A PUBLICATION OF THE CENTER FOR ACTION AND CONTEMPLATION

◆ SPECIAL EDITION ◆

ORDER
DISORDER
REORDER

CAC Publishing
Center for Action and Contemplation
cac.org

"*Oneing*" is an old English word that was used by Lady Julian of Norwich (1342–1416) to describe the encounter between God and the soul. The Center for Action and Contemplation proudly borrows the word to express the divine unity that stands behind all of the divisions, dichotomies, and dualisms in the world. We pray and publish with Jesus' words, "that all may be one" (John 17:21).

EDITOR:
Vanessa Guerin

ASSOCIATE EDITOR:
Shirin McArthur

PUBLISHER:
The Center for Action and Contemplation

ADVISORY BOARD:
David Benner
James Danaher
Ilia Delio, OSF
Sheryl Fullerton
Stephen Gaertner, OPraem
Ruth Patterson

Design and Composition by Nelson Kane

Oneing
An Alternative Orthodoxy

The biannual literary journal of the Center for Action and Contemplation.

Oneing is a limited-edition publication; therefore, some editions are no longer in print. To order available editions of *Oneing*, please visit https://store.cac.org/.

Oneing

VOLUME 8 NO. 2

Every reform becomes its own new orthodoxy and the painful pattern of growth begins all over again.

—Richard Rohr

RICHARD ROHR FIRST introduced the concept of "Order, Disorder, Reorder" at a conference sponsored by the Center for Action and Contemplation (CAC). As faculty member and Dean of the Center's Living School, he later presented it as part of the student curriculum.

In his article "Include and Transcend"—which is adapted from the preface to his book *The Wisdom Pattern: Order, Disorder, Reorder*—Rohr describes the often-recurring pattern of order, disorder, reorder in the following way.

- Order, by itself, normally wants to eliminate any disorder and diversity, creating a narrow and cognitive rigidity in both people and systems.

- Disorder, by itself, closes us off from any primal union, meaning, and eventually even sanity in both people and systems.

- Reorder, or transformation of people and systems, happens when both are seen to work together.

Rohr follows these three descriptions with an outline "which illustrates how the great spiritualties and philosophies often taught this quite directly, but with different vocabularies, symbols, and metaphors."

The CAC's four additional faculty members—Cynthia Bourgeault, James Finley, Barbara Holmes, and Brian McLaren—were each invited to contribute an article that explored Rohr's concept of order, disorder, reorder within the context of their unique ways of teaching and their own "vocabularies, symbols, and metaphors." Additionally, Kirsten Oates, the CAC's Managing Director of Planning and Programs, was invited to include a brief statement together with her clarifying diagram of Rohr's dynamic concept.

In her article, Cynthia Bourgeault provides examples to help the reader further understand the three principles. She explains the metaphysical pattern of the Law of Three, or three forces, which she calls "affirming, denying, and reconciling." She states that "the essence of the Law of Three is the stipulation that every phenomenon, on whatever scale (from subatomic to cosmic) and in whatever world, springs from the interaction of three forces: the first active, the second passive, and the third neutralizing."

James Finley invites the reader to reflect on Rohr's concept of order, disorder, reorder "as an aphorism, . . . words of wisdom that embody the transformative process of learning to live in an habitual, underlying awareness of and response to God's presence in our lives" by way of a journey of love through profound poetic "spiritual depth dimensions." He uses powerful analogies to usher the reader beyond ego consciousness through "fidelity to meditation" to the place where "no matter how badly we have trashed ourselves in treating ourselves in the hurtful ways we are treated, [the] intimately realized pearl [of great price] remains un-trashed and undiminished in any way for it is that in us that belongs completely to God."

Barbara Holmes takes a quite different approach in her article, "Emerging Wisdom Patterns in the Black Lives Matter Movement," where she argues in her first header that we are called to be "Disrupting the 'Order' that Is Killing Us"—referring to Black, Indigenous, and People of Color (BIPOC). She names numerous Black men and women elders who have fought and died for justice and freedom. Holmes observes, "We believed that our efforts to bring about racial justice were linear. There was a goal straight ahead and if we kept working at it, we would eventually grasp the brass ring and declare victory." She goes on to write, "As Fr. Rohr points out, that is not how the world works. Wisdom patterns of order, disorder, and reorder are found throughout our lives. Change is not the result of a beeline toward the goal; instead, patterns prepare the way."

Brian McLaren concludes this edition using the vocabularies and metaphors of "fictional narrative." He cleverly explains order, disorder, and reorder through a lecture by his story's protagonist, a college science professor who "explained that his purpose was to make clear the current transition from modernity to postmodernity by comparing it to . . . 'our last major transition, the medieval-to-modern transition which occurred around 1500.'" McLaren's tale echoes wisdom from Rohr's article, in which he states that "the human preference for binary thinking has kept us from seeing that when history evolves with a new idea, cultural mood, or consciousness, we need not (dare not, actually!) completely exclude the previous idea, mood, or consciousness."

The CAC is indeed blessed to have such marvelous thinkers working collectively to teach rich concepts from their own unique perspectives. May you find deep value in this Special Edition of *Oneing*, which showcases the voices of the CAC faculty.

Vanessa Guerin
Editor

CONTRIBUTORS

RICHARD ROHR, OFM, is a Franciscan priest of the New Mexico Province and the Founding Director of the Center for Action and Contemplation in Albuquerque, New Mexico. An internationally recognized author and spiritual leader, Fr. Richard teaches primarily on incarnational mysticism, non-dual consciousness, and contemplation, with a particular emphasis on how these affect the social justice issues of our time. Along with many recorded conferences, he is the author of numerous books, including *The Universal Christ: How a Forgotten Reality Can Change Everything We See, Hope For, and Believe* and *The Wisdom Pattern: Order, Disorder, Reorder*. To learn more about Fr. Richard Rohr and the CAC, visit https://cac.org/richard-rohr/richard-rohr-ofm/.

REV. CYNTHIA BOURGEAULT is a modern-day mystic, Episcopal priest, writer, and internationally known retreat leader. Cynthia divides her time between solitude at her seaside hermitage in Maine and global teaching to spread the recovery of the Christian contemplative and wisdom path. She is the founding Director of both the Contemplative Society and the Aspen Wisdom School. She is the author of numerous books, including *The Holy Trinity and the Law of Three, The Meaning of Mary Magdalene, The Wisdom Jesus, Centering Prayer and Inner Awakening, Mystical Hope, The Heart of Centering Prayer*, and *Love Is the Answer*. To learn more about Cynthia Bourgeault, visit https://cynthiabourgeault.org/.

DR. JAMES FINLEY is a contemplative teacher and writer and a retired clinical psychologist. He has led retreats throughout the United States and Canada, attracting men and women from all religious traditions who seek to live a contemplative way of life in the midst of today's busy world. Early in his life, James lived as a cloistered monk at the Trappist monastery of the Abbey of Gethsemani in Kentucky, where the world-renowned monk and author Thomas Merton was his spiritual director. James is the author of *Merton's Palace of Nowhere, The Contemplative Heart,* and *Christian Meditation: Experiencing the Presence of God.* To learn more about James Finley, visit https://jamesfinley.org/.

Kirsten Oates is an alumna of the Center for Action and Contemplation's Living School and the CAC's Managing Director of Planning and Programs. She has experience in strategic consulting with Bain & Company and the Bridgespan Group, as well as a number of nonprofit and faith-based organizations. She spent seven years as Director of Strategy for City Church San Francisco, California. Kirsten grew up in Australia and graduated from the Australian National University in Canberra with a Bachelor's Degree in Economics and a Bachelor of Laws with Honors. Kirsten Oates lives with her husband in Sausalito, California.

Dr. Barbara Holmes received a Doctor of Philosophy in Religion (Ethics) from Vanderbilt and also holds degrees in divinity, sociology, theater arts, education, and law. She is a spiritual teacher and writer focused on African American spirituality, mysticism, cosmology, and culture. Barbara says, "My life is committed to the struggle for justice, the healing of the human spirit, and the art of relevant and radical creativity." She has worked with homeless missions, HIV/AIDS support groups, and international ministries in Kenya and Japan. Barbara's most recent publications include *Dreaming, Liberation and the Cosmos: Conversations with the Elders; Joy Unspeakable: Contemplative Practices of the Black Church;* and *Race and the Cosmos.* Learn more about Dr. Holmes at https://www.drbarbaraholmes.com/.

Brian McLaren advocates and works toward "a new kind of Christianity"—just, generous, and working with people of all faiths for the common good. Brian began his career as a college English teacher and then served as a pastor for twenty-four years. He now writes, speaks, and engages in contemplative activism, focused on caring for the planet, seeking justice for the poor, and working for peace. Brian's books include *A Generous Orthodoxy; Why Did Jesus, Moses, the Buddha, and Mohammed Cross the Road? We Make the Road by Walking;* and *The Great Spiritual Migration.* To learn more about Brian McLaren, visit https://brianmclaren.net/.

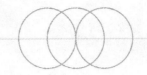

ORDER

DISORDER

REORDER

Please Call Me by My True Names

Don't say that I will depart tomorrow—
even today I am still arriving.

Look deeply: every second I am arriving
to be a bud on a Spring branch,
to be a tiny bird, with still-fragile wings,
learning to sing in my new nest,
to be a caterpillar in the heart of a flower,
to be a jewel hiding itself in a stone.

I still arrive, in order to laugh and to cry,
to fear and to hope.

The rhythm of my heart is the birth and death
of all that is alive.

I am the mayfly metamorphosing
on the surface of the river.
And I am the bird
that swoops down to swallow the mayfly.

I am the frog swimming happily
in the clear water of a pond.
And I am the grass-snake
that silently feeds itself on the frog.

I am the child in Uganda, all skin and bones,
my legs as thin as bamboo sticks.
And I am the arms merchant,
selling deadly weapons to Uganda.

I am the twelve-year-old girl,
refugee on a small boat,
who throws herself into the ocean
after being raped by a sea pirate.
And I am the pirate,
my heart not yet capable
of seeing and loving.

I am a member of the politburo,
with plenty of power in my hands.
And I am the man who has to pay
his "debt of blood" to my people
dying slowly in a forced-labor camp.

My joy is like Spring, so warm
it makes flowers bloom all over the Earth.
My pain is like a river of tears,
so vast it fills the four oceans.

Please call me by my true names,
so I can hear all my cries and my laughter at once,
so I can see that my joy and pain are one.

Please call me by my true names,
so I can wake up,
and so the door of my heart
can be left open,
the door of compassion.

—Thich Nhat Hanh[1]

Let me keep surrendering my self
until I am utterly transparent.

—Psalm 19

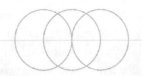

Include and Transcend

By Richard Rohr

THE HUMAN PREFERENCE for binary thinking has kept us from seeing that when history evolves with a new idea, cultural mood, or consciousness, we need not (dare not, actually!) completely exclude the previous idea, mood, or consciousness.

We grow best by including what was good and lasting in the previous stage and avoiding the overreaction and rebellious spirit that have characterized most revolutions up to now. This demands both *humility and the capacity for non-dual thinking*, qualities that are rare in most zealots, reformers, and revolutionaries. Slash-and-burn only creates a whole new set of things to correct or rebel against in the long haul. Either-or thinking creates disjunction and mistrust immediately. Both-and thinking creates continuity and trust over time.

This nonviolent compromise can most simply be stated as *include and transcend*. It is at the core of what we mean by wisdom and by nonviolence.

As it applies here, we can trust and even need certain kinds of "disorder" to clarify what our original "order" meant, lacked, or intended. There are always a few needed correctives to every new proposition—and those correctives only appear over time and with practice. Thus, we have amendments to our original American Constitution—and now, some think that these also need to be amended. Every reform becomes its own new orthodoxy and the painful pattern of growth begins all over again. Yes, this is the rub of evolution, like the grinding of tectonic plates.

If we can rightly achieve an integration of original plan plus correctives, rule plus "the exception that proves the rule," order plus disorder, we have what I am calling *reorder!* And this is good—at least for a while. Reorder moves us forward in a positive way, but then sets the stage for the pattern to continue all over again. Even good reorder, in time, becomes its own faulty, yet canonized, order and its own cracks will begin to show. The need for humility and creativity never stops. This pattern must have been much easier when the human lifespan was forty years, but, at age seventy-seven, I have gone through this cycle at least four good times.

Order, by itself, normally wants to eliminate any disorder and diversity, creating a narrow and cognitive rigidity in both people and systems.

Disorder, by itself, closes us off from any primal union, meaning, and eventually even sanity in both people and systems.

Reorder, or transformation of people and systems, happens when both are seen to work together.

In my book *The Wisdom Pattern*, I shared an outline which illustrates how the great spiritualties and philosophies often taught this quite directly, but with different vocabularies, symbols, and metaphors:

* Native peoples called it the cycle of Day ▶ Night ▶ Sunrise or
Sun ▶ Moon ▶ Sun or
Summer ▶ Fall ▶ Winter ▶ Spring.

Every reform becomes its own new orthodoxy.

- Scientists speak of star ❭ supernova explosion ❭ vast amounts of light and energy.

- World Mythologies present stories of Journey ❭ Fall ❭ Return to a new home.

- Religions often use some form of Birth ❭ Sin ❭ Rebirth or Law ❭ Failure ❭ Forgiveness or all is okay ❭ catastrophe ❭ hope.

- The Bible presents it as Garden of Eden ❭ Fall ❭ Paradise.

- Walter Brueggemann teaches three kinds of Psalms: Psalms of Orientation ❭ Psalms of Disorientation ❭ Psalms of New Orientation.[1]

- There are three sections to the Hebrew Scriptures: Law ❭ Prophets ❭ Wisdom.

- Speakers and writers often refer to three steps forward and two steps backward.

- Johann Fichte (1762–1814) called it thesis ❭ antithesis ❭ synthesis.[2]

- George Ivanovich Gurdjieff (1866–1949) called it Holy Affirming ❭ Holy Denying ❭ Holy Reconciling.[3]

- Philosophy speaks of Classic or Essentialism ❭ Postmodern or Existentialism or Nihilism ❭ Process or Evolutionary Philosophy.

- Chemistry illustrates the pattern through solution ▶ dissolution ▶ resolution.

- Paul Ricœur (1913–2005) spoke of First Naïveté ▶ Complexity ▶ Second Naïveté[4] or First Simplicity (dangerous) ▶ Recalibration ▶ Second Simplicity (enlightened).

- The Recovery movement speaks of Innocence ▶ Addiction ▶ Recovery.

- Many now just speak generally of construction ▶ deconstruction ▶ reconstruction.

- Christians call it Life ▶ Crucifixion ▶ Resurrection.

G IVEN THE PREVALENCE of this recurring theme, it must now be considered culpable blindness that most people still consider it somewhat of a surprise, a scandal, a mystery, or something to be avoided or overcome by an easy jump from stage one (order) to stage three (reorder). This is human hubris and illusion. Progress is never a straight and uninterrupted line, but we have all been formed by the Western Philosophy of Progress that tells us it is, leaving us despairing and cynical.

So, what does this demand of leaders and teachers? More than anything else, humility and creativity! These virtues offer the detach-

Reorder moves us forward in a positive way, but then sets the stage for the pattern to continue all over again.

ment and patience that allow history to move forward because they keep our absolutes, our certitudes, and our obstinacy out of the way. Even God submits to mercy and forgiveness toward "what used to be." Apparently, God enjoys doing this because it never stops happening: Every original "order" (and I do think I mean "every") learns to include an initially threatening disorder, which morphs into and creates a new reordering, and we begin all over again. . . . ◆

Before I had studied Ch'an for thirty years, I saw mountains as mountains, and rivers as rivers. When I arrived at a more intimate knowledge, I came to the point where I saw that mountains are not mountains, and rivers are not rivers. But now that I have got its very substance, I am at rest. For it's just that I see mountains once again as mountains, and rivers once again as rivers.

—Qingyuan Weixin

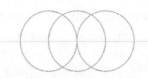

The Law of Three

By Cynthia Bourgeault

EMBEDDED WITHIN THE theological formula that Christians recite mostly on automatic pilot ("in the name of the Father, the Son, and the Holy Spirit") lies a powerful metaphysical principle that could change our understanding of Christianity and give us the tools so long and so sorely needed to reunite our shattered cosmology, rekindle our visionary imagination, and cooperate consciously with the manifestation of Jesus' "Kingdom of Heaven" here on earth. That principle is called the Law of Three, and the metaphysics that derive from it can be called "ternary metaphysics."

While inklings of it can be discerned in certain Christian mystical streams (particularly those flowing through Jacob Boehme [1575–1624] and Pierre Teilhard de Chardin [1881–1955]), it was articulated only in the early twentieth century by the Armenian-born spiritual teacher G. I. Gurdjieff (1866–1949), and until very recently it has been studied and transmitted exclusively within that stream of contemporary esotericism known as the Gurdjieff Work.

In every new arising there are three forces involved:
affirming, denying, and reconciling.

THE ESSENCE OF the Law of Three is the stipulation that every phenomenon, on whatever scale (from subatomic to cosmic) and in whatever world, springs from the interaction of three forces: the first active, the second passive, and the third neutralizing. In the language of the Gurdjieff Work, these are known respectively as "Holy Affirming, Holy Denying, and Holy Reconciling," or "affirming, denying, and reconciling (or neutralizing)," or simply "first, second, and third."

The most important thing to keep in mind here is that this third force is an *independent* force, coequal with the other two, not a *product* of the first two as in the classic philosophy of "thesis, antithesis, synthesis." Just as it takes three independent strands of hair to make a braid, so it takes three individual lines of force to make a new arising. This third force serves to bring the other two forces (which would otherwise remain disconnected or deadlocked) into relationship, from which forward momentum can emerge.

You can see how this principle underlies these examples. The opposition of wind and keel will not push a sailboat forward through the water; it takes the "reconciling" presence of the helmsperson to create the new phenomenon: the course made good over the water. The seed will not sprout simply by being placed in the earth (even moist earth); it is sunlight that catalyzes the action. James Moore (1929–2017) offered a trio of other examples, all familiar to students of the Work: "Flour and water become bread only when bonded by fire; plaintiff and defendant have their case resolved only through a judge; nucleus and electrons constitute an atom only within an electromagnetic field." [1]

All three forces are *equally important* participants in the unfolding of a new arising.

*Affirming, denying, and reconciling are not fixed points
or permanent essence attributes but can and do
shift and must be discerned
situationally.*

T HIS ASPECT OF the Law of Three takes some getting used
to for most Western minds, conditioned as we are to think in
terms of great binary opposites with fixed archetypal charac-
teristics. It is difficult to hear the terms *active/passive* and not immediately translate as "masculine/feminine." It's equally difficult to avoid
imputing a value judgment: affirming force is "good"; denying force is
"bad." But both of these well-engrained mental habits will make it very
difficult to grasp the novelty of the idea that Gurdjieff is presenting
here. If you fall into the trap of seeing holy affirming as the masculine
principle or of equating holy denying with the obstacle to be overcome, then you will have missed the powerful new leverage the Law
of Three has to bring to our traditional notions of process and change.
It is precisely for this reason, to avoid old trains of association, that
many students of the Work prefer to identify these three forces simply
as "first, second, and third."

The first all-important implication to be drawn from this model is
that all three forces are *equally important* participants in the unfolding
of a new arising. Denying (second force) is never an obstacle to be
overcome but always a legitimate and essential component of the new
manifestation. In and of itself this realization brings a radically new
orientation to problem solving. The "enemy" is never the enemy but
a necessary part of the "givens" in any situation, and solutions will
never work that have as their goal the elimination of second force. As
in Jesus' famous teaching in Luke 14:28 — "For what king, going out
to war against another king, will not sit down to consider whether he
with ten thousand is able to oppose the one who comes against him
with twenty thousand?"—resistance must be factored in: not simply
to cover one's bases but because it is an indispensable ingredient in
the forward motion.

The second, and equally profound, implication here is that
"affirming, denying, and reconciling" are *roles*, not identities, and
they reveal themselves only situationally. For any situation to move
forward, all three must be present, and the accuracy with which one
is able to assign the roles is a critical component in the solution of any

problem. Often a situation that appears to be at an impasse can be shifted simply by interchanging the roles. A shift in any one of the terms will immediately affect the other two.

This point was well illustrated by Maurice Nicoll (1884–1953) in his celebrated example of "the Work as Neutralizing Force."[2] In the unawakened human being, according to Nicoll, personality is active, essence is passive, and life itself is the Neutralizing (third) force—or, in other words, life conspires to keep a person just where they are: conditioned, superficial, and in Gurdjieff's unlovely estimate, "a machine." When that person commits themselves to a path of awakening and places the Work in the position formerly occupied by unconscious living, a change begins to take place: personality ceases to run the show and the person's real but heretofore latent essence begins to emerge as the active force. It is this flexible, shape-shifting capacity of the three forces that is primarily responsible for the Law of Three's intrinsic dynamism.

Solutions to impasses generally come by learning how to spot and mediate third force, which is present in every situation but generally hidden.

I F WE OBSERVE a stoppage in anything, or an endless hesitation at the same point," P. D. Ouspensky (1878–1947) wrote, it is because "the third force is lacking."[3] From what we have seen already about the Law of Three, this point should now be obvious, since the third, or neutralizing, force is what brings the other two into relationship. No third force, no action. It is worth reemphasizing the consequences of this principle in terms of orienting oneself toward enlightened action: it does no good whatsoever simply to align oneself with one of the two opposing forces in an attempt to overcome the other; a solution will appear only when third force enters. The Gurdjieff equivalent of Buddhist "skillful means" implies attuning oneself always to third force and striving to midwife it in the situation at hand.

The problem is that third force is not that easy to attune to; in fact, according to virtually every writer in the Gurdjieff tradition, perhaps most succinctly summarized by Jacob Needleman: "Third force is invisible to human beings in the ordinary consciousness in which they live."[4] This is not because it is in and of itself so subtle and rarified

The capacity to recognize and consciously mediate third force belongs to what we would now call unitive or nondual consciousness.

(although some Work teachers do indeed tend to portray it that way) but because the default setting of our usual consciousness is skewed toward the binary, toward "either/or." It lacks both the sensitivity and *the actual physical capacity* to stay present to third force, which requires an established ability to live beyond the opposites. This capacity does not belong to our usually "formatory" mind, as Gurdjieff called it—that is, our egoic operating system, with the tendency to think in facile and conditioned "thought bytes." It is only attained through persistent efforts toward conscious awakening, effected through practices that reorient the mind and strengthen the nervous system to be able to bear the higher vibrational frequency of what Gurdjieff calls "objective truth." In the conceptual map more familiar in our own times, the capacity to recognize and consciously mediate third force belongs to what we would now call unitive or nondual consciousness, and its stabilization in a person reflects an evolutionary advance in consciousness.

The Work tradition is by no means of one mind in its understanding of third force. To those writers of a more mystical inclination, it seems itself to be an inbreaking of a higher order of reality (akin to what Christians might call grace); to others, it appears more the case that this inbreaking of a higher reality simply opens a person's eyes to the third force that is actually there already but hidden. Perhaps the truth lies somewhere in between: Whatever the actual mechanics may be, the bottom line is that third force does not enter a situation automatically; it requires the conscious mediation of an alert presence and a flexible intelligence. The cultivation of these two capacities comprises the primary practical business of the Work.

The opposition is never the problem.

T HE SINGLE MOST liberating insight to come out of our collective work with the Law of Three was the realization that what appears to be the resisting or opposing force is never actually the problem to be overcome. Second force, or holy denying, is a legitimate and essential component in every new arising: *no resistance, no new arising!*

That realization in and of itself radically rearranges the playing field, shifting the focus away from trying to eliminate the opposition and toward working collaboratively for a more spacious solution. According to the Law of Three, once an impasse has constellated, it can never be solved by going backward but only forward, into that new arising that honors all the players and brings them into a new relationship. (Albert Einstein [1879–1955] seems to have been on to this insight in his famous dictum that a problem can never be solved at the level at which it is created.) The three forces are like three strands in a braid; all three are required for the weaving.

One woman in our group was almost instantly able to turn around a very difficult standoff with an ultraconservative bishop when she realized that his resistance was not the problem to be solved but a given to be worked with. With an almost visceral "Aha!" she relaxed her sense of polarization and was stunned to learn the next day that he had miraculously softened his stance. While it was not clear to her who in the chancery office had actually been the broker of third force here, it was clear to her that the two relaxations were not unrelated.

One can only imagine how greatly the political and religious culture wars of our era could be eased by this simple courtesy of the Law

The resisting or opposing force is never actually the problem to be overcome.

of Three: (1) the enemy is never the problem but the opportunity; (2) the problem will never be solved through eliminating or silencing the opposition but only through creating a new field of possibility large enough to hold the tension of the opposites and launch them in a new direction. Imagine what a different world it would be if these two simple precepts were internalized and enacted. •

"The Law of Three" is an adapted excerpt from Cynthia Bourgeault, The Holy Trinity and the Law of Three: Discovering the Radical Truth at the Heart of Christianity, © 2013, pages 2–3, 25–26, 28–33, 39–40. Reprinted by arrangement with Shambhala Publications, Inc., Boulder, Colorado. www.shambhala.com.

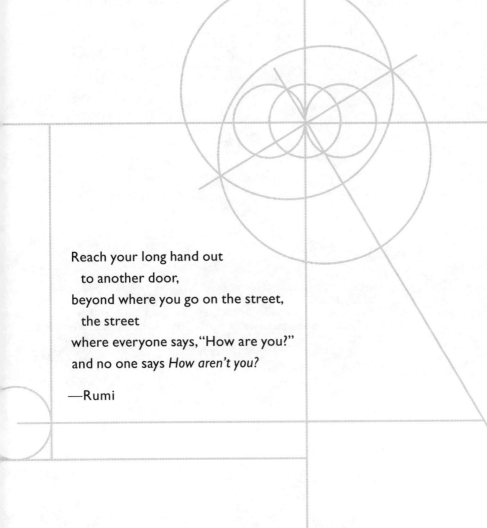

Reach your long hand out
   to another door,
beyond where you go on the street,
   the street
where everyone says, "How are you?"
and no one says *How aren't you?*

—Rumi

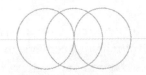

Order, Disorder, Reorder:

A Contemplative Aphorism of Spiritual Wisdom

By James Finley

I N THIS ARTICLE, I am inviting you to join me in reflecting on Richard Rohr's *order, disorder, reorder* as an aphorism, which is to say, as words of wisdom that embody the transformative process of learning to live in an habitual, underlying awareness of and response to God's presence in our lives.

The transformative process of order, disorder, and reorder flows on and on in endlessly varied ways, in the daily realities of parenting, and in giving ourselves over to poetry, art, and all creative processes. It occurs in all the ways we seek to serve and help those less fortunate than ourselves, as well as in the lives of those we serve. And, as we shall be focusing on in the reflections offered here, this transformative process of order, disorder, and reorder is a way of bearing witness to the intimate interiority of religious conversion.

While keeping these far-ranging realms of human experience in mind, I will limit myself here to a poetic exploration of the spiritual depth dimensions of order, disorder, and reorder that occur in the midst of nature, in marital love, and in the art of healing.

◆◆◆

To begin exploring the interior dimensions of order, disorder, and reorder as the process occurs in the midst of nature, imagine you are wading ankle deep along the ocean shore. In your customary orderly experience of yourself in ego consciousness, it is true you are just ankle deep. It is true that if you head out into deeper water it will get plenty deep soon enough. And it is true that as you enter by incremental degrees into the ocean's depths, the depths you are entering have been measured in finite, objective terms that science provides.

But now imagine that, as you look out at the ocean's vast expanse, you are given over to an inner reverie, in which you are led to wonder something you have never wondered before: What if the ocean in its hidden center is infinitely deep? And what if the ocean is infinitely giving the infinite depths of itself away, whole and complete, in and as each incremental degree of entrance into abyss-like depth?

In giving yourself over to this interior stance of sustained attentiveness, an intimate and radical reordering of your understanding begins to emerge within you as you begin to realize that yes, it is true that, in your finite experience of yourself in ego consciousness, you

This transformative process of order, disorder, and reorder is a way of bearing witness to the intimate interiority of religious conversion.

really are wading ankle deep along the ocean shore. And yet, at a qualitatively more interior, spiritual level, you are given to realize that, as you wade ankle deep along the ocean shore, you are in water way over your head. In a subtle and delicate manner that you cannot and do not need to explain, your awakening heart knows, senses that the ocean embodies God's oceanic presence in which you "live and move and have [your] being" (Acts 17:28).

As the aura of this graced awareness dissipates, you are able to discern a previously unrecognized disorder that was present within yourself prior to your awakening. This disorder pertains to an illusion you harbored about yourself, insofar as you went about imagining that your finite experiential understanding of yourself in ego consciousness had the final say in who you are and are called to be.

In the light of the unitive mystery to which you have been fleetingly awakened, you know that yes, you are ego, sure enough. But at the qualitatively more interior level to which you were fleetingly awakened, your finite ego self is realized to be the opening through which a unitive mystery accessed you, leaving you feeling blessed, grateful, and amazed to live in the world that embodies the generosity of God.

This fleeting taste of unitive consciousness gives birth to a desire to abide in the depths so fleetingly glimpsed. And this desire to abide in the fulness of presence to which you have been awakened brings with it the realization of the need to undergo a *reordering* of the attitudes and habits of mind and heart needed to bring you into an ever more habitual state of attunement with the unitive mystery to which you have been awakened.

◆◆◆

I NOW INVITE YOU to join me in reflecting on how Richard Rohr's aphorism of order, disorder, and reorder occurs in the spiritual, transformative dimensions of marital love. We can begin by pausing to wonder why married couples, who have been blessed with many years of loving and being loved by each other, never tire of reminding each other of the first time they saw each other—why they find renewed delight each time they recall the first time they touched, the first time they kissed, the first time they began to realize they were falling in love with each other.

Is it not because, from their present vantage point of being so well seasoned in the ways of love, they are able to realize that, as they look back at their first faltering gestures in the ways of love, that they were, unbeknownst to them at the time, already in water way over their heads?

As time goes by, they have learned to recognize that the most simple and unassuming events in their life together can suddenly become yet another graced opportunity to access and be accessed by love's mysterious ways. To see how this is so, imagine a married couple having a conversation they have had many times, as they go over the chores that need tending to in the week ahead. As their discussion comes to a close, she tells him that this might not be the best time to go into it, but that she wants to share with him insights she has been having about their relationship. He tells her this would be a good time for him and that he wants to hear what she has to say.

Notice that, as she begins to speak of their relationship, she is not simply moving on to a new item on the list of items they have been discussing. It is not that there is the dental appointment, getting the oil changed in the car, and then there is their relationship. For their relationship is a qualitatively more interior topic that requires that they reorder their minds and hearts in ways that are commensurate with the non-objective, interior realms of their love for each other.

She begins by saying that what has been occurring to her lately is a renewed sense of amazement and gratitude in realizing that before they met, she did not know that the kind of love they have for each other was even possible.

He responds, telling her this is true for him as well.

"The thing is," she says, "our love has become so deep."

He nods in agreement, letting her know he is one with her as she speaks.

Then, without consciously knowing what she is going to say next, she says, "I wonder if we will ever get to a depth of love so deep that there will not be a yet deeper depth of love to get to."

See what she is pondering? She is wondering if there is an end to love. In the moment of attentive wondering her question evokes, the level of consciousness at which they began their loving exchange begins to yield to a qualitatively enriched awareness of the depths of love in which they are making their descent.

"I wonder if we will ever get to a depth of love so deep that there will not be a yet deeper depth of love to get to."

• ◆ •

I CALL THIS SUBTLE transformative event an *axial moment* because the level or quality of their experiential understanding at which they began conversation begins to turn, as on an hidden axis, drawing them down into a qualitatively deeper, more interior experience of the oneness with abyss-like depths of love into which they are making their descent. In the language of Richard Rohr, their conversation at this point embodies the transformative process of reordering their experience and understanding in accordance with the transformative process that is occurring within them as they yield to the boundaryless nature of love.

Staying a bit longer with the married couple in the midst of their transformative encounter, something even more wondrous might be granted to them as they begin to sense that the abyss-like depth of love into which they are descending is welling up and giving itself to them whole and complete in and as this moment of their loving union with each other.

This awareness is likely to be too delicate and subtle, too overwhelmingly immediate, to be experienced in a full-blown conscious manner. But, in some intimate and obscure manner, they can sense that the abyss-like mystery of love in which they are making their descent is welling up and giving itself away whole and complete in and as the intimate immediacy of this moment of their renewed awareness of the gift and miracle of their love for each other.

Insofar as this occurs, we might say they are becoming momentary mystics in realizing that God is the infinity of this intimately realized state of their transsubjective communion. And the intimate immediacy of their transsubjective communion is the incarnate infinity of God. And in this intimate and interior way, they realize their marriage to be a sacramental embodiment of Richard Rohr's aphorism of the *Universal Christ*.

The understanding of transcendence posited by the philosopher Martin Heidegger (1889–1976) can, hopefully, help us to explore the graced reordering of our minds and hearts that we are now attempting to explore. Heidegger understood transcendence as that which actively surpasses all set limits. With this in mind, what if the married couple, in their moment of intimate awakening, were to draw a circle around the unitive mystery of love in which they are in this moment so unexplainably immersed? Is it not so that no matter how big they would make that circle, the fullness of love they are experiencing would breach the circumference of that circle and would do so playfully and effortlessly, as that which love delights to do?

And what might the married couple do in the aftermath of such graced visitations of love which they are, from time to time, so privileged to experience? They might continue talking in a shared awareness that the nuanced meanings of their words embody and sustain their deepening communion, which transcends what words can say. Or they might become silent, being silenced in this depth of love. Or they might make love or hold hands, or they might burst out laughing, or they might have lunch. And what are these ways of being together, if not ways of sustaining their immersion in the lingering aura of a reordering of their experiential understanding of love as a mystery that utterly transcends, even as it utterly permeates, the chores and demands of the day with a felt sense of an inherent value that cannot be calculated?

We must now acknowledge the challenging fact that, just as poets are powerless to force the evocative language of poetry out onto the blank page, just as those committed to healing are powerless to make healing happen, so too, lovers are powerless to force their way into

Often when we least expect it, there it is again—that longing we do not understand for that union we do not understand, but which we know is real because we have experienced it.

moments of oceanic communion that transcend the finite ego and all the ego can attain. By that, I mean that they cannot make these moments happen by the sheer brute force of their finite efforts in ego consciousness.

But what the married couple can eventually learn to do, in a process of trial and error, is to freely choose to assume the interior stance that offers the least resistance to being overtaken by the graced plenitude of love's mysterious ways. As they learn to assume this interior stance, they discover that the graced moment of oceanic oneness which they are powerless to attain, attains them in their powerlessness to attain it.

◆◆◆

I T SEEMS TO me that this is a helpful way to understand the transformative, reordering power of fidelity to meditation, as any act faithfully entered into with all our heart, that takes us to the deeper place. The importance of fidelity to meditation, understood in this foundational sense, becomes apparent each time the lingering aura of graced awakenings dissipates, leaving us once again overtaken by the momentum and demands of daily life that close off experiential access to the deeper place that we know and sense to be the homeland of our awakened hearts. We can sense that, as each graced visitation dissipates as mysteriously as it came, it leaves behind a desire to abide in the depths so fleetingly glimpsed.

At first, this desire is like a flame that flickers in the wind—in all the ways it seems to disappear altogether in the momentum of the days' demands. Then, often when we least expect it, there it is again—that longing we do not understand for that union we do not understand, but which we know is real because we have experienced it.

And so it is that we are pleased to discover that fidelity to meditation practice reorders the habitual, underlying patterns of our minds and hearts in accordance with the art of freely choosing that interior stance in which the fullness of presence we are powerless to attain, attains us in our powerlessness to attain it.

If the interior quickening of our mind and heart occurred while walking along the ocean shore, our fidelity to walking along the ocean shore becomes our meditation practice. If the graced awakening occurred in the pause between two lines of a poem, freely choosing to pause between two lines of a poem becomes our practice. In this same way, as moments of spiritual awakening occur in moments of marital intimacy, a married couple's fidelity to their moments of being mutually present and vulnerable with each other becomes for them a meditation for two.

◆◆◆

A s a way to conclude our poetic explorations, we can turn our attention to the ways the transformative process of order, disorder, and reorder occur in the interpersonal realm in which we as human beings move from ego-based to more spiritually based ways to help each other heal from suffering. Turning our attention to healing in this context is important because suffering arises in the very realms in which we seek to find happiness and fulfillment. Not every marriage survives the painful upheavals that can tear a marriage apart. Not every parent is fortunate to have a child who is physically and emotionally healthy. Not everyone who has had to endure traumatizing events is able to move beyond the ongoing, internalized effects of the trauma that fester within them as psychological symptoms that embody suffering.

In endlessly varied ways, our innate sense of order, of inner peace, which occurs in the loving and safe conditions of daily life, is thrown into the disorder that suffering brings into our lives. When this happens, we seek to engage in the healing process in which disorderly states of suffering are healed in ways that restore the sense of wholeness and well-being that has been lost. Certainly, our faith inspires and guides this healing process in which we, as human beings, discover how true it is that, in risking to share what hurts the most in the presence of someone who will not invade us or abandon us, we can learn not to invade or abandon ourselves.

As we move along the horizontal path of our passage through time, in which incremental realizations of healing and wholeness occur, the vertical depth dimensions of deep healing that spirituality brings into our lives can begin to well up out of the hidden depths of the healing encounter. This radicalized reordering emerges within us in realizing that when we risk sharing what hurts the most in the presence of someone who will not invade or abandon us, we can discover within ourselves what Jesus called the pearl of great price, the invincible preciousness of ourselves in the midst of all that is most broken within ourselves and within all who live with us on this earth.

To draw upon the imagery of Thomas Merton, the pearl of great price is that in us which is not subject to the brutalities of our own will. For no matter how badly we have trashed ourselves in treating ourselves in the hurtful ways we are treated, this intimately realized pearl remains un-trashed and undiminished in any way for it is that in us that belongs completely to God. No matter what has been done to us in the past, and no matter how broken and confused it might have left us, the pearl of great price continues to shine within us as that in us which no one can diminish or destroy, for it is that in us which belongs entirely to God, waiting to be discovered, accepted, lived, and shared with others, day by day.

The field in which this pearl is hidden is the inner landscape of our own life. And the great price paid to make this pearl our own is revealed to us in the mystery of the cross—which, in this context, can be understood as the lifelong process of dying to our dreaded and cherished illusions that anything less than an infinite union with infinite love will put to rest the restless longing of our minds and hearts. And the mystery of the cross, so understood, goes on to reorder our most intimate understanding, bringing us to the intimate realization that we are loved through and through and through with an invincible love that is infinitely more real than the imagined authority of our wayward ways, so that, even as we continue to sweep up the pieces in tending to all that still needs tending to, we do so grounded in a peace that is not dependent on the outcome of our efforts. For the peace that sustains us is the peace of God on which everything depends. Learning to understand ourselves in this way allows us to understand everyone in this way, inspiring us and empowering us to be a healing presence in an all-too-often traumatized and traumatizing world.

I hope that what has been offered here helps you to understand how Richard Rohr's aphorism of order, disorder, and reorder helps us to understand how mysteriously we are being transformed in ever-deeper realizations of the one life that is at once God's and our own. May each of us continue to grow in this graced understanding, knowing and trusting that this transformative and divinizing process will continue to sustain and guide us, up to and including the moment of our death—and beyond.

Amen. So be it. •

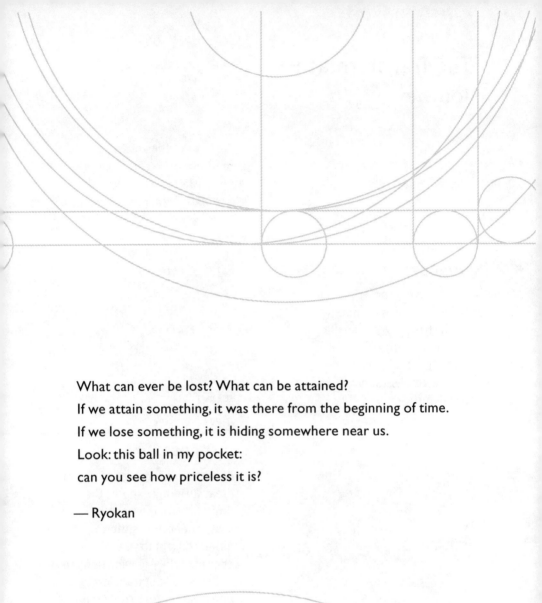

What can ever be lost? What can be attained?
If we attain something, it was there from the beginning of time.
If we lose something, it is hiding somewhere near us.
Look: this ball in my pocket:
can you see how priceless it is?

— Ryokan

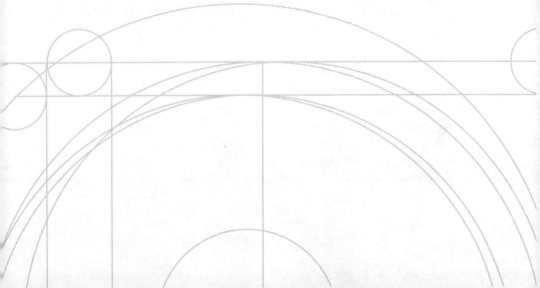

The Transformative Journey

LOVE

There is an Ultimate Reality (God or Love) manifest in all things. This love is the engine for and destination of our transformation.

ORDER

We begin by ordering our lives around our finite self which is caught in an illusion of separateness from Love. The finite self focuses on separateness, survival, and self-sufficiency.

DISORDER

An encounter with great love or great suffering exposes the limitations of the finite self and is experienced as suffering. We either consent to this experience in faith — leaving us open to the process of transformation — or return to the ordering around the finite self.

REORDER

A mysterious and graced experience of God's presence can be tasted and increasingly frees the will to be aligned with God's will for the love and healing of the world.

Growth and Transformation

By Kirsten Oates

A t the Center for Acton and Contemplation, we believe that growth and transformation come from more fully inhabiting all of reality—the seen and the unseen, the finite and the infinite. This diagram seeks to capture Richard Rohr's teaching that the universal pattern of reality is captured in the gospel narratives of Jesus' life, death, and resurrection. This pattern is applied to our lives, not in a linear fashion, but cyclically, and it is experienced in ways of knowing as well as not knowing, in an ever-deepening transformation into Love. Growth is nurtured by a daily practice of surrendering to God through prayer or meditation, where we can experience God's presence in our suffering and our joy. This connection to God leads us to become an active presence of love in solidarity with the suffering of the world. In our final surrender to God in death, we will know completely the reality of the seen and unseen and be fully transformed into the Love that, from the very beginning, was our destiny. •

Hold on to what you believe,
Even if it's a tree that stands by itself.
Hold on to what you must do,
Even if it's a long way from here.

—Crowfoot

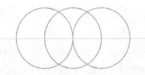

Emerging Wisdom Patterns in the Black Lives Matter Movement

By Barbara Holmes

A universal pattern can be found in all societies and, in fact, in all of creation. We see it in the seasons of the year; the stories of Scripture; the life, death, and resurrection of Jesus; the rise and fall of civilizations; and even in our own lives. . . .

We are indeed "saved" by knowing and surrendering to this universal pattern of reality. Knowing the full pattern allows us to let go of our first order, trust the disorder, and, sometimes even hardest of all—to trust the new reorder. Three big leaps of faith for all of us, and each of a different character.

—Richard Rohr

DISRUPTING THE "ORDER" THAT IS KILLING US

LIVING IN AMERICA in a black or brown body requires courage and resilience. I approach the issue of wisdom patterns in the Black Lives Matter Movement (BLMM) from this embodied perspective. As I write, I can hear the elders in my family discussing injustice in this country. One uncle says, "If the lawmakers and law enforcers are out of order, if the law is not just, then it is not law. Order is as order does." I know what he means.

What does law and order mean when the "order" of things allows police officers to kill unarmed, handcuffed black and brown people at will? What does it mean when the "order" that purportedly guides our social contract is infused with racism, xenophobia, and ethnocentrism? When our laws require the separation of infants and toddlers from their parents at the Mexican border, is this still considered "order"?

As a nation, the United States has not lived up to the soaring rhetoric of its (slaveholding) founders. Instead, the country clings to its mythologies about rugged individualism and patriotism, while ignoring its history of colonization and its abuse of indigenous communities. Moreover, America's infatuation with whiteness—a category of power, privilege, and protection—still threatens the lives of all Black, Indigenous, and People of Color (BIPOC).

Although my parents sheltered me as much as they could from the realities of racism, we lived in New Haven, Connecticut, an activist community. With Yale in our backyard, an activist pastor, and Black Panther members in our youth fellowship group at church, I soon developed a passion for justice. The only reason that I did not become a Black Panther was because of my curfew. Their meetings were too late. My Dad let us change as much of the world as we wanted, as long as we did it before 7:00 p.m. After that time, everyone had to be in the house.

After Bloody Sunday, when Martin Luther King, Jr. (1929–1968) called for everyone to come to Selma for the second march, my Dad and I boarded a bus and headed for Alabama. Our silent march to Montgomery felt like spiritual order to me. We were creating order with our dignity and communal resolve, and we believed that legislation which codified our demands for justice would be the culmination of our activism.

We believed that our efforts to bring about racial justice were linear. There was a goal straight ahead and if we kept working at it, we would eventually grasp the brass ring and declare victory. As Fr. Rohr points out, that is not how the world works. Wisdom patterns of order, disorder, and reorder are found throughout our lives. Change is not the result of a beeline toward the goal; instead, patterns prepare the way.

And so, here we are in the year 2020, trying to process the murder of George Floyd (1973–2020)—a murder as heinous as the murder of Emmett Till (1941–1955). In his last essay, John Lewis (1940–2020) wrote,

> Emmett Till was my George Floyd. He was my Rayshard Brooks, Sandra Bland and Breonna Taylor. He was 14 when he was killed, and I was only 15 years old at the time. I will never ever forget the moment when it became so clear that he could easily have been me. In those days, fear constrained us like an imaginary prison, and troubling thoughts of potential brutality committed for no understandable reason were the bars.[1]

The difference between Till's and Floyd's deaths is that Floyd's death could not be dismissed, downplayed, or denied, because a brave young woman filmed it on her cellphone. We all watched as an officer of the law and representative of an "order" that prioritizes the protection of white bodies, pressed his knee into Floyd's neck until he was dead.

Without a clear understanding of wisdom patterns, it might seem that history is repeating itself. We might conclude, erroneously, that the efforts and sacrifices of Black elders were in vain: C.T. Vivien, John Lewis, Rosa Parks, Joseph Lowry, and Ella Baker, to name a few. Some, who transitioned recently, lived long enough to see the resurgence of racism in its most virulent form and the resistance of yet another generation in the BLMM.

For too long, we have pretended that there was no "order" to the racism that has been killing us.

For too long, we have pretended that there was no "order" to the racism that has been killing us. We were told that there are always "bad apples" among good folks. Each incident was approached as aberrant behavior and not as the systematic enforcement of white supremacy. Finally, because of the death of George Floyd, the rise of BLMM, and the recent death of John Lewis, allies and enemies alike are seeing the structural realities and the historical scaffolding of injustice that makes change a cyclical reality.

THE BLESSED NECESSITY OF DISORDER

> Until the killing of black men, black mothers' sons [and daughters], becomes as important to the rest of the country as the killing of a white mother's sons [and daughters], we who believe in freedom cannot rest until this happens.
>
> —Ella Baker

IN THIS FAMOUS quote, Ella Baker (1903–1986), civil rights activist and organizer, reminds us of the reason that we continue the struggle for justice: it is for fairness and equal treatment under the law. Another generation is on the rise, and they are confronting police brutality and advocating for Black lives through the BLMM.

The BLMM: Another Generation
Responds to a Racist Order

THE BLMM was inspired when unarmed Black teen Trayvon Martin (1995–2012) was killed with a bag of candy and a soda in his hands. His murder was traceable to his hoodie, his skin color, and an over-zealous gun-toting neighborhood-watch vigilante. The acquittal was expected; the response to the tragedy was not.

The shot that killed Trayvon Martin reverberated throughout the nation, stirring another generation into action. Trayvon wasn't the first young Black person to die because of the projection of criminality on all youth of color, but when the incident occurred, the fatigue and anger of the community were at an all-time high. As the body count rose daily, fair-minded people recoiled in horror. Black bodies bled in the streets with such regularity that it took our collective breath away.

There seemed to be no logic for the carnage, from traffic stops to the sale of a single cigarette. Bullets shattered not just the bodies of victims, but, also, any sense of safety or illusion of belonging for the African American community. We had become complacent. So many decades had passed since the Civil Rights Movement (CRM) that we thought it was safe to take our place in a nation where the seized and stolen immigrant and refugee were purportedly welcomed. And then the carnage began again, as the systems of the dominant culture tried to re-impose its order on BIPOC.

Hashtag for Justice

IN THE AFTERMATH of Trayvon's death, three self-proclaimed queer women are credited with the launch of the BLMM: Alicia Garza, Patrice Cullors, and Opal Tometi. The phrase Black Lives Matter appeared for the first time on Facebook in July of 2013.[2] In a "Love Letter to Black Folks," Alicia Garza wrote, "I continue to be surprised at how little Black lives matter. And I will continue that. Stop giving up on black life ... black people. I love you. I love us. Our lives matter."[3]

Garza's friend Patrisse Cullors created the hashtag #blacklivesmatter and the resurgence was underway. It would prove itself to be a movement grounded in crisis contemplation. The frequent deaths were devastating, but the response had to be peaceful and purposeful. It's important to discuss the state of Black communities when Trayvon was killed, because the incidents that fueled the birth of the BLMM include very specific social, religious, and political factors.

The State of the Black Union before Trayvon

URBAN BLACK COMMUNITIES were staggering toward the future after the infusion of drugs during the 1980s and the rise of gang violence during the 1990s. No one seemed to understand the relationship between the increase in gang activity and the rising incarceration of Black men and women. With the dissolution of family came the substitution of morally skewed gang loyalty and support, and the increase of violence, poverty, and health crises in the cities.

In response to the demand for justice, systems morph and adjust while maintaining the status quo. Certainly, there were enough sacrifices, martyrs, and legislation during the 1960s to ensure justice for all. Yet, Ephesians 6:12 reminds us that the battle for justice is spiritual: "We wrestle not against flesh and blood but against powers and principalities." These powers and systems do everything they can to resist change.

So public hangings end and the murders of unarmed Black folk rise. Slavery ends, but mass incarceration of minority populations increases. Jim Crow practices are no longer openly discriminatory; they reappear as educational and economic disparities, voter suppression, and aggressive police actions against people of color and culture.

The election of President Barack Obama inspired optimism and looked like real change in a racist "order." Yet, just days before Obama's inauguration, transit police officer Johannes Mehserle shot Oscar Grant in the Fruitvale BART Station in Oakland.[4] Perhaps Grant's death was an omen of things to come. Instead of a post-racial atmosphere of commonality and support, Obama took office as his opponents in Congress vowed to see him fail.[5]

Violence against black and brown bodies continued to be part of the normal "order" of this nation, but change was on the horizon. Differences included the 24-hour news cycle, social media, cellphone cameras, and the sudden glare of media attention. As the deaths of unarmed Black people continued, it would not be the Civil Rights generation who would respond to the tragedy. Although aging CRM activists muttered their frustration at obligatory press conferences, it was the millennial generation on social media that sparked the resistance.

BLMM: Not Your Grandmother's Civil Rights Movement

As the millennials will tell you, "This is not your grandmother's Civil Rights Movement." They are right. Although both the CRM and BLMM seek the betterment of life for Black people and their communities, and resist oppression with contemplative practices and activism, they use different strategies and leadership models and seek different goals.

Comparing Leadership Models

The central contradiction of the CRM was that it was a quest for democracy led by organizations that frequently failed to function democratically.[6]

THE BLMM is a decentralized network of local organizations. The leadership model is grassroots and communal. Patrice Cullors, a founder of the BLMM, says, "We are not leaderless, we are leader-full."[7] The benefits of a leader-full movement are immediately apparent. It is difficult to infiltrate, undermine, or disrupt an organic movement that draws its power from regenerating communal cells. Like Ella Baker, the BLMM rejects the "single charismatic" male leadership model in favor of a diffused, independent, and grassroots model.

BLMM's organization is more like the Student Nonviolent Coordinating Committee (SNCC) than "all the king's men" and their hierarchical inner circle.[8] Baker was a capable and effective organizer. Moreover, she embodied the contemplative practices central to the CRM. Contemporaries described her "as contemplative to a fault."[9]

Her participatory leadership model implicitly followed the wisdom pattern. She trusted the people to understand their situation and to resist the order that was being imposed. She taught them how to sustain one another in the midst of chaos and disorder as they worked for transformation with integrity. As for her male colleagues in the CRM, Baker had real concerns about the lack of egalitarian processes and the transference of hierarchical structures from the church to the streets that kept women activists at the margins of power.[10]

As Baker knew, change is not the easy culmination of dedicated activism. There would be necessary disorder before the groundwork was laid for transformation and rebirthing. The BLMM is nonviolent but confrontational, peaceful, but unwilling to accept the status quo.

Violence against black and brown bodies continued to be part of the normal "order" of this nation, but change was on the horizon.

The most important directive of Black Lives Matter is to deal with anti-Black racism.

The BLMM replaces the charismatic male figure with many voices. It invites the gifts of the community and the emergence of local leaders. Each chapter of the BLMM decides on local priorities while sharing and participating in the creation of ultimate goals. And now, the torch is being passed from one generation to another.

Coming full circle during the summer of 2016, SNCC issued their support for the BLMM, stating,

> With their protests and demands, the Movement for Black lives is continuing to exercise their rights, guaranteed to all Americans under the First Amendment of the United States Constitution. We, the still-active radicals who were SNCC, salute today's Movement for Black lives for taking hold of the torch to continue to light this flame of truth for a knowingly forgetful world![11]

Similarly, during John Lewis' last days, he stood in Black Lives Matter Plaza, motionless and in a contemplative stance. He seemed to be looking beyond the disorder, the protests in Portland against the abuses of federal officers, who were trying to reimpose the old order. He stood contemplating all of the good trouble on display that the next generation was getting into. He said, "That's why I had to visit Black Lives Matter Plaza in Washington D.C., though I was admitted to the hospital the following day, I just had to see and feel it for myself, that after many years of silent witness, the truth is marching on."[12]

"DISORDERING" AT THE BEHEST OF THE SPIRIT

IN RESPONSE TO the violence and anti-Black racism, the BLMM disrupts everyday life. They block traffic and refuse to allow "business as usual." The response is not riot or violence; it is the twenty-first-century version of the sit-in. CRM activists got parade permits and stayed along the side of the road so as not to interfere with traffic. BLMM activists "shut it down" with song, putting their bodies on the line. They have blocked bridges and routes to the airport during holidays, interfered with marathons, and protested in the Mall of America one year, refusing to let Christmas shopping go on as usual after the murder of Jamar Clark in Minneapolis. Their demands leave very little wiggle room.

The respectability politics of the Black church and the CRM had as a primary strategy the proof of worthiness to be included and fully accepted as citizens and human beings. The BLMM is not concerned with respectability as a strategy. This is not to say that the activists are not "respectable"; it is that they will not prove through their behavior, dress, or assimilation their worthiness to be treated as human beings.

> As a social movement, Black Lives Matter can be understood as growing out of a specific opposition to respectability politics by insisting that regardless of any ostensibly non-respectable behavior . . . their lives matter and should not be treated with deadly force.[13]

Respectability politics has deep roots in the Black church, but it was part of a survival agenda that few remember. Historically, the Black church served as the lens through which a carefully crafted image of African Americans as fully human was presented to the public. Performance of humanness in the public square through dress, speech, education, and consumer choices is an artifact of a perilous past.

When lynching was normal and there was no safety anywhere for black bodies, it was critical that activists present an image of respectability, a look and a sound that middle America recognized as "normal and human." The politics of respectability was not a lazy sellout option; it was a small "spoke in the wheel" of genocide.[14] The image of Rosa Parks in white gloves, hat, and suit, refusing to leave her seat, sent messages to dominant culture that she did not fit the images in their mythologies about blackness. It unsettled the enforcers of segregation and, by the grace of God, she was not harmed.

Today, the times require a different response to oppression and violence against black bodies. Today, the most respectable image that young protesters can offer is through their authenticity, resolute voices, and pride in community and culture. Accordingly, the BLMM is a complete disruption of the political playbook that prevailed during most of the justice movements. The BLMM uses disruption for transformation rather than the predictable politeness and political compromises that were part of the ordinary negotiations of prior generations of social activists.

The goals of the movements are also very different. The CRM by necessity had to address the legal impediments to full citizenship. Accordingly, "rights" specific to the denials encoded in Jim Crow laws were the priority: i.e., education, integration, voting, housing, etc. The BLMM focuses on the denial of Black humanity by the systems structured to support oppression. And while the legal system is again the object of scrutiny, more often the cry for justice is a direct demand to "stop killing us."

It is more than direct talk. The BLMM is not trying to gain respect or white support by saying what White America wants to hear. In the words of BLMM leader Brittany Packnett, "Black people for too long have been forced to refine our message according to what is comfortable for the mainstream. We have made a distinctive choice not to do it.... Our goal is to be free and authentic, not to pacify others."[15]

The decision to live authentically through their actions and rhetoric is not just a strategy to defeat oppression. It is one of the most contemplative responses to injustice available. Howard Thurman (1899–1981) urged us to listen to the genuine within ourselves. Living authentically requires accessing deep communal and personal resources. The disorder that follows "order" is the fertile ground for rebirthing. The activism need not be neat and orderly, polite or comforting to whiteness. All it needs to do is rise from and be responsive to the needs of the people. It needs to be attuned to a spiritual reality that offers the potential for the soon-coming of peace, love, and community.

REORDERING AND TRANSFORMING THROUGH RELENTLESS JOY

S o, GIVEN ALL that has happened, where is the joy? The CRM found its joy in the rallies that preceded marches. They sang themselves happy and were in one accord as they faced violence with peace. For the BLMM, I saw one example of joy as resilience at the funeral of Jamar Clark (1991–2015).

When I moved from Memphis to accept the presidency of United Theological Seminary of the Twin Cities, in a suburb of Minneapolis, I wondered what path my activism would take. In a predominantly

The disorder that follows "order" is the fertile ground for rebirthing.

white, liberal state, I expected that most of the work for justice was done or being done. So, I settled in to lead the institution, only to realize that young men and women were dying from police violence in New York, Baltimore, Texas, Ferguson, and in the liberal state of Minnesota. In Minneapolis, Jamar Clark was killed by the police under questionable circumstances.

The funeral was held at Shiloh Temple International Ministries. The church was packed with young people wearing tee shirts emblazoned with poignant messages and the image of the deceased. Uncomfortable politicians sat on the platform while teens texted and tweeted in their seats.

On the day of the funeral, the BLMM-led protest at the police station was still going on. After the funeral, we left the church to go to the site of the protest because the funeral procession was scheduled to drive through the area. People sang and distributed food, and then we heard the honking horns of the hearse.

> To sing and dance one's way out of the pit of the American Empire is constitutive of black religion. The zeitgeist of resistance that permeates our music, dance, poetry, style and movement through time and space is a nonmaterial response to material conditions.[16]

The funeral procession entered the tight pathway surrounded by BLMM activists and allies. Every few feet, a door of a funeral car would be flung open and the occupants would jump out and dance as if their lives depended on the movement. Hip hop music blasted from the cars. The respect being paid was primal and authentic. They were performing authenticity and grief so profound that only feet could speak. Our hearts were breaking, our feet were moving, and there was joy unspeakable and full of glory.

No person or community can be healthy in a constant state of resistance. There must be respite, celebration, and relief. Without this respite, post-traumatic injuries contribute to intra-communal conflict. These symptoms are then used by the dominant culture as proof that oppression is necessary and justified.

In response, we heal ourselves in community through our contemplative practices, praying together, dancing together, and caring for one another. We have joy because no bullet aimed at Martin, or Malcolm or John or Bobby, or Jamar or Eric, or Sandra, or Trayvon can stop us. And while we celebrate, we will be our authentic selves. You can't kill us and then tell us to wear a tie. You can't kill us and tell us to follow your rules of etiquette.

T HIS IS A revolution of the people. Our elders got us this far by faith and now the revolution will be televised. It will be stomped to rap music and maybe our clothes won't match, and that's all right. Some of us are homeless, some of us have records, some of us are educated, some of us are not. But none of us can breathe. What better place to declare our freedom—our determination that, if one falls, another will take her place—than in honor of one whose breath was taken without cause.

Personally, I am tired. I don't want my sons to have to address this same state-sanctioned sadism in the future—and no, I am not expecting anything to change because Aunt Jemima and Uncle Ben are taken off of the pancake and rice boxes. I am not placated by the NFL's offer to play the Negro National Anthem at every game. Instead, I am convinced that we need to look directly at the spiritual forces and wisdom patterns at play.

We are tired, but the struggle for justice is intergenerational and the millennials are "woke." In the words of Reinhold Niebuhr,

> Nothing that is worth doing can be achieved in our lifetime; therefore we must be saved by hope. Nothing which is true or beautiful or good makes complete sense in any immediate context of history; therefore we must be saved by faith. Nothing we do, however virtuous, could be accomplished alone; therefore we are saved by love. No virtuous act is quite as virtuous from the standpoint of our friend or foe as it is from our standpoint. Therefore we must be saved by the final form of love which is forgiveness.[17]

Reinhold Niebuhr's words ring true. Although we wish it were otherwise, the struggle for justice is never completed in one lifetime or one rebellion. The shifting of systems, the turning of hearts, the forgiveness of oppressions and the dissipation of anger (righteous or not) takes time.

It is not easy to confront injustice. But, as God is our witness, we are ready to be free by any peaceful means necessary. I don't know what "success" will look like, but I know that it will require solidarity and the regrettable, but inevitable, loss of life. The only way forward is with contemplative activism that feeds the soul and encourages the community.

We will not be discouraged by our journey "through the blood of the slaughtered."[18] Instead, we exude life, we express our joy and the affirmation, "we gonna be alright."[19] We have disrupted the "order" that was killing us, while we embrace the disorder which is the fertile microcosm for our transformation. Thanks be to God!

When historians pick up their pens to write the story of the 21st century, let them say that it was your generation who laid down the heavy burdens of hate at last and that peace finally triumphed over violence, aggression and war. So I say to you, walk with the wind, brothers and sisters, and let the spirit of peace and the power of everlasting love be your guide.
—John Lewis, July 30, 2020

ASHE and AMEN

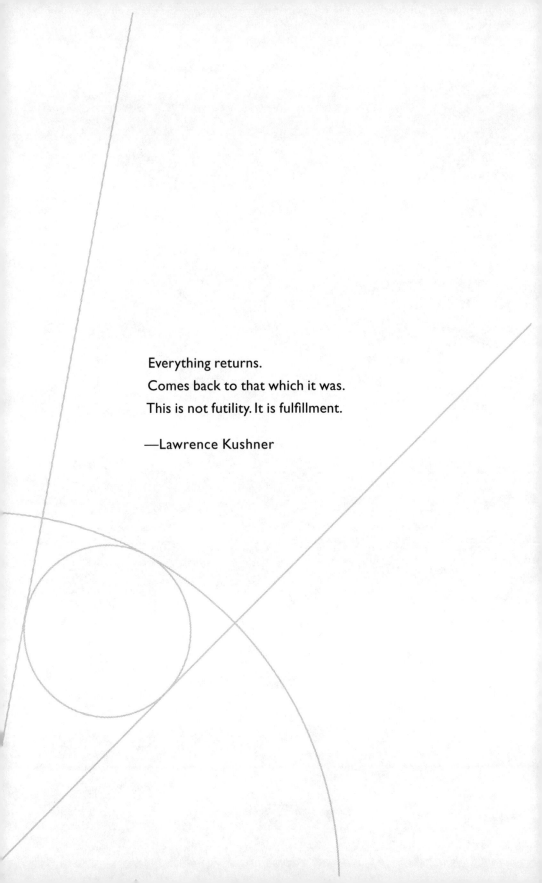

Everything returns.
Comes back to that which it was.
This is not futility. It is fulfillment.

—Lawrence Kushner

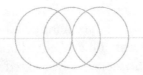

Looking Back
to Look Ahead

By Brian D. McLaren

WAY BACK IN 2001, I released a book called *A New Kind of Christian*. Two critical moments affected the shape of the book. First, I was about one hundred pages into my first draft and realized that I was only about ten percent through my outline. At that rate, I would write a book so long that nobody would ever read it! Second, I recalled something a reviewer had said about my first book, *The Church on the Other Side*. "If McLaren is serious," this reviewer wrote, "he should be writing fiction, drama, and poetry, because what he's trying to convey can't simply be conveyed by normal non-fiction prose." Those two realizations came together, I hit "delete" on everything I had written and started over, rewriting my book as a fictional narrative. It became the first volume of a trilogy that was recently republished by Fortress Press.

In Chapter 4 of the book, a young pastor (the narrator of the book, Rev. Dan Poole) attends a lecture at a local college by his daughter's high school science teacher, Dr. Neil Edward Oliver (nicknamed Neo for his initials). Dr. Oliver is a committed Christian, and his lecture invites Dan to venture out of his inherited order, to risk disorder, in a quest for a new and better order. I've edited the chapter slightly for use here. Dan Poole introduces the lecture and inserts a few comments, but otherwise, this excerpt is Dr. Oliver's lecture.

◆◆◆

NEO'S LECTURE HAD a kind of scholarly feel to it, complete with visuals on an old overhead projector (which, by the way, drove me crazy; it had a bad fan that interrupted his lecture randomly with an ugly grinding screech, the kind of metal-on-metal sound that makes your skin crawl). He was much less animated and much more serious than he had been with me in the bagel shop. He explained that his purpose was to make clear the current transition from modernity to postmodernity by comparing it to the last major historical transition. His love of history really came through.

"One of the best ways to get perspective on the scope and significance of the current postmodern transition," Neo said, "is to go back to our last major transition, the medieval-to-modern transition which occurred around 1500.

"The year 1500 works as a transition point to the modern era for a number of reasons. Consider the confluence of world-changing events that occurred around 1500." Neo fiddled with the projector for a few seconds and then, after getting it to work without screeching, had to chase his transparency—which had slid gracefully off the projector and under a desk. Finally, he got his visual centered on the screen. It looked like this:

General Category	Specific Event
1. New communication technology, with profound effects on how people learn, think, and live.	The printing press revolutionizes human culture.
2. New scientific worldview, with staggering implications for humanity.	Copernicus asserts that the earth is not the center of the universe, toppling the medieval model of the universe.
3. A new intellectual elite emerges, challenging church authority and introducing a new epistemology (way of knowing).	Galileo, Newton, Bacon, and others give birth to modern science.
4. New transportation technologies increase the interaction of world cultures around the globe, making the world seem smaller.	The development of the caravel (sailing ship) for long voyages makes possible the explorations of the late thirteenth to early sixteenth centuries.
5. Decay of an old economic system and rise of a new one.	Market capitalism replaces feudalism.
6. New military technology.	Development of modern guns leads to the development of the modern infantry and rise of modern nation-state.
7. New attack on dominant authorities, with defensive reaction.	Protestant Reformation denies authority of Roman Catholic Church; Counter-Reformation develops in response.

"Now," Neo continued, "think of the similar confluence of changes clustering around the year 2000." This time he managed to switch transparencies without mishap. Notice that the items in the left-hand columns are exactly the same as before.

General Category	Specific Event
1. New communication technology, with profound effects on how people learn, think, and live.	Radio and television, and then the computer and the Internet, revolutionize human culture.
2. New scientific worldview, with staggering implications for humanity.	Post-Einsteinian theories of relativity, quantum mechanics, indeterminacy, and the expanding universe unsettle the stable, mechanistic worldview of modern science; psychology, psychiatry, neuropsychology, and psychopharmacology create new ways of seeing ourselves and new crises in epistemology.
3. A new intellectual elite emerges, challenging church authority and introducing a new epistemology (way of knowing).	Postmodern philosophy challenges all existing elites and deconstructs existing epistemologies.
4. New transportation technologies increase the interaction of world cultures around the globe, making the world seem smaller.	The development of air travel leads to the trivialization of national borders and intensifies the interaction of world cultures.
5. Decay of an old economic system and rise of a new one.	The global economy transforms both communism and capitalism, and the immanent development of e-commerce suggests further market revolution.
6. New military technology.	Air warfare and nuclear weapons change the face of warfare, and the new threats of terrorism (especially chemical and biological), power-grid sabotage, and cybercrime begin to revolutionize the role of governments in keeping the peace.
7. New attack on dominant authorities, with defensive reaction.	Secularism, materialism, and urbanism contribute to the decline of institutional religion worldwide; fundamentalist movements arise in reaction and self-defense.

Neo read his chart before driving his point home. "Obviously, our whole view of the medieval world flows from our perspective as moderns—the word *medieval* itself simply meaning 'middle period,' what came between the ancient world and now. And obviously, medieval people never thought of themselves as medieval, any more than Plato thought of himself as an ancient. Thus, the very term *medieval* reminds us that our modern perspective is only that: a perspective, a point of view, not the ultimate perspective, not *the* point of view. But it's hard for us to really feel the impact of that obvious truth, immersed as we are in our own modern worldview.

"Sometimes, the best way to see what it means to be modern is to try to reverse the perspective and put ourselves into the shoes and minds of medieval people—instead of seeing them through our eyes, to try to see the world through their eyes, thus creating a vantage point from which to get a new view of ourselves. C. S. Lewis takes on this extraordinary challenge in one of his least-appreciated books *The Discarded Image*. He explains that medieval European Christians had developed a sophisticated worldview that was so intertwined with their faith that to them it was an essential part of their faith. In this worldview, the universe consisted of a series of concentric spheres, the smallest of which was the earth. As spheres ascended from the earth, they held objects of increasing perfection—the moon, then the planets, then the stars, the angels, and so on. The spheres moved around the earth in a beautiful kind of cosmic dance, and, it was thought that as they moved, they produced a beautiful music, symbolic of the harmony of God's creation.

"Near the end of the book, Lewis notes how new developments—especially new observations in the field of astronomy, which are of special interest to me as a science teacher—forced the medieval model of the universe to be 'adjusted,' and the adjustments were becoming increasingly complex. Here's how Lewis explains this tinkering with the model:

THE OLD SCHEME . . . had been tinkered a good deal to keep up with observations. How far, by endless tinkerings, it could have kept up with them till even now, I do not know. But the human mind will not long endure such ever-increasing complications if once it has seen that some simpler conception can 'save the appearances' [i.e. account for the data]. Neither theological prejudice nor vested interests can permanently keep in favor a Model which is seen to be grossly uneconomical.[1]

"In other words," Neo explained, "the medieval world had developed a working worldview, a working model of reality—a paradigm, a mental map—that could not account for or adapt to increasing amounts of new data (like the scientific findings of Copernicus, and later Galileo, and of course, later still, Darwin). Perhaps like a contract or constitution that is updated with more and more footnotes, fine print, and other amendments, people try to keep the old contract alive, but eventually the amendments outweigh the original document, and someone says, 'Why don't we just start over from scratch on a new one?'

"But it's not that easy. Trading in an old model of reality for a new one has real costs associated with it. True, something may be gained, but a lot is lost too. Let me put on the overhead this quote from Lewis, where he starts making clear what was at stake in trading in the old worldview for a newer one.

> IN OUR UNIVERSE [the earth] is small, no doubt; but so are the galaxies, so is everything—and so what? But in theirs there was an absolute standard of comparison. The furthest sphere, Dante's *maggio corpo*, is, quite simply and finally, the largest object in existence.... Hence to look out on the night sky with modern eyes is like looking out over a sea that fades away into mist, or looking about one in a trackless forest—trees forever and no horizon. To look up at the towering medieval universe is much more like looking at a great building. The 'space' of modern astronomy may arouse terror or bewilderment or vague reverie; the spheres of the old present us with an object in which the mind can rest, overwhelming in its greatness but satisfying in its harmony.... Pascal's terror at *le silence éternel de ces espaces infinis* [the eternal silence of the infinite spaces] never entered his mind. He is like a man being conducted through an immense cathedral, not like one lost in a shoreless sea.[2]

"So," Neo intoned, "it was not comfortable, it was not easy, being pushed out of the medieval world by the hard data of the new emerging science. One became, in a sense, spiritually homeless. But as we know, eventually the trade was made. We gave up the medieval

What if we live at the end of the modern period, at a time when our modern world-view is crumbling, just as the medieval one began to do in the sixteenth century?

worldview with its harmonious, concentric spheres, its absolute up and down, its ultimate finite boundaries. We accepted a model that was less personal, to be sure, and also less orderly in some ways, but even more rigidly controlled in others. As part of the trade, we gave up the idea that some people simply had the God-given right to rule over others, and we gave up our corresponding respect for 'the authorities.' As a result, authoritative tradition lost much of its value, and we unleashed five centuries of a kind of change that the medievals wouldn't have understood very well—we call it 'progress' or 'evolution,' but to them it would have sounded like chaos and insanity. To them, change was considered ungodly, since God was changeless. Their conservatism was perhaps further bolstered by the belief that the best days on earth—back in the Garden of Eden—were behind them, not ahead of them. Changing that static and past-oriented worldview to a dynamic and future-oriented one wouldn't come easy.

"That brings me to an important question for you to think about: Is it possible that we as moderns have similarly intertwined a different but equally contingent worldview with our eternal faith? And another question: What if we live at the end of the modern period, at a time when our modern worldview is crumbling, just as the medieval one began to do in the sixteenth century?

"Let me go back to C. S. Lewis again. He seemed to anticipate these kinds of questions with his characteristic brilliance. At the end of *The Discarded Image*, he does something quite astounding for a somewhat conservative writer in the early 1960s: He begins to suggest that our modern view itself is not the absolute, ultimate truth, that it is not the ultimate viewpoint but rather just a 'view from a point.' It is as if his success at entering the medieval world has enabled him to see his own modern model of the universe in the same way we might look at a model of a car: maybe the best model so far, but not the absolute best model that will ever exist. Lewis, usually thoroughly modern, writing late in life sounds himself almost postmodern.

"Most modern people love to relativize the viewpoints of the others against the unquestioned superiority of their own modern viewpoint. But in a way, you cross the threshold into postmodernity the moment you turn your critical scrutiny from others to yourself, when you relativize your own modern viewpoint. When you do this, everything changes. It is like a conversion. You can't go back. You begin to see that what seemed like pure, objective certainty really depends heavily on a subjective preference for your personal viewpoint. In this next quote, Lewis makes exactly these very postmodern moves, and emphasizes how one's subjective posture affects what one sees and 'knows objectively':

> IT WOULD ... be subtly misleading to say, "The medievals thought the universe to be like that, but we know it to be like this." Part of what we now know is that we cannot, in the old sense, "know what the universe is like" and that no model we can build will be, in that old sense, "like" it. ... There is no question here of the old Model's being shattered by the inrush of new phenomena. The truth would seem to be the reverse; that when changes in the human mind produce a sufficient disrelish of the old Model and a sufficient hankering for some new one, phenomena to support that new one will obediently turn up. I do not at all mean that these new phenomena are illusory. Nature has all sorts of phenomena in stock and can suit many different tastes.[3]

"Lewis then continues with these reflections not on the medieval model of the world, but on our modern one, and on models in general:

> I HOPE no one will think that I am recommending a return to the Medieval Model. I am only suggesting considerations that may induce us to regard all Models in the right way, respecting all and idolizing none. We are all, very properly, familiar with the idea that in every age the human mind is deeply influenced by the accepted Model of the universe. But there is a two-way traffic; the Model is also influenced by the prevailing temper of mind. We must recognize that what has been called "a taste

in universes" is not only pardonable but inevitable. We can no longer dismiss the change of Models as a simple progress from error to truth. No Model is a catalogue of ultimate realities, and none is a mere fantasy. Each is a serious attempt to get in all the phenomena known at a given period, and each succeeds in getting in a great many. But also, no less surely, each reflects the prevalent psychology of an age almost as much as it reflects the state of that age's knowledge. Hardly any battery of new facts could have persuaded a Greek that the universe had an attribute so repugnant to him as infinity; hardly any such battery could persuade a modern that it is hierarchical.[4]

"Lewis then concludes his book with this fascinating prediction:

IT IS NOT IMPOSSIBLE that our own Model will die a violent death, ruthlessly smashed by an unprovoked assault of new facts—unprovoked as the nova of 1572. But I think it is more likely to change when, and because, far-reaching changes in the mental temper of our descendants demand that it should. The new Model will not be set up without evidence, but the evidence will turn up when the inner need for it becomes sufficiently great. It will be true evidence. But nature gives most of her evidence in answer to the questions we ask her. Here, as in the courts, the character of the evidence depends on the shape of the examination, and a good cross-examiner can do wonders. He will not indeed elicit falsehoods from an honest witness. But, in relation to the total truth in the witness's mind, the structure of the examination is like a stencil. It determines how much of that total truth will appear and what pattern it will suggest.[5]

"What Lewis imagined to be 'not impossible' some generations away—the death of the modern model or worldview—turns out to be happening just a single generation after he wrote." Here Neo paused and looked up from his notes and gave the students a long gaze, making eye contact with nearly every one.

"The modern worldview, including the modern version of Christianity that you follow, bears ominous resemblances to the medieval worldview that Lewis so crisply described, the worldview that was celebrated and embodied in the medieval cathedral. The ornateness,

I want you to invest your lives not in keeping the old ship afloat but in designing and building and sailing a new ship.

grand construction, and sheer size of medieval cathedrals mirrored the complexity and expansiveness of the medieval worldview itself. However, both the cathedrals and the worldview they expressed reached a point where they permitted no new development and where they threatened to collapse under their own weight. Not only that, but over time they were nearly as difficult to maintain as they were to build. Ironically, the very stone buildings that expressed the belief that their medieval version of Christendom would last forever now mock that belief because today, when we visit them in Europe, they seem to us like museums—or mausoleums. They tell a story of a world that is over.

"There is one last thing that I want to say to you before I finish. This is the real point of my whole talk, actually. You are college students, with a long life ahead of you, so full of potential and promise. You may disagree with me, but I believe that the modern version of Christianity that you have learned from your parents, Sunday School teachers, and even from your campus ministries is destined to be a medieval cathedral. It's over, or almost over.

"Most of your peers live in a different world from you. They have already crossed the line into the postmodern world. But few of you have. Why? Because you want to be faithful to the Christian upbringing you have received, which is so thoroughly enmeshed with modernity. One of the most important choices you will make in your whole lives will be made in these few years at this university. Will you continue to live loyally in the fading world, in the waning light of the setting sun of modernity? Or will you venture ahead in faith, to practice your faith and devotion to Christ in the new emerging culture of postmodernity?

"I don't think you'll hear many people my age urging you to do what I'm about to urge you to do. But I will say it boldly: I want you to invest your lives not in keeping the old ship afloat but in designing and building and sailing a new ship for new adventures in a new time in history, as intrepid followers of Jesus Christ. Thank you."

◆◆◆

T HE CHAPTER ENDS with Dan Poole observing, "Frankly, I expected some applause. It had been a good lecture, if a little long and overly philosophical in the middle. I found the ending downright inspiring. But there was nothing. Just silence. A tense silence."

What I wrote almost twenty years ago seems even more apropos today. Whether we're Protestant or Catholic, we can observe so many of our leaders obsessing over some things (abortion, LGBTQIA+ equality, all-male leadership, inerrancy or infallibility of religious authorities) while remaining largely oblivious to others (institutionalized racism, police brutality, destruction of the planet, gross economic inequality, the proliferation of weapons, etc.). They seem to be living in a different universe. In a sense, they are, and they are desperate to keep it afloat because it's all they know: It's the fading modern universe of white supremacy, colonialism, patriarchy, and environmental plunder for profit.

The responsibility will fall to folks like you and me to doubt the assumptions of that "old world order" and venture out of it. Once out, we must inhabit disorder with open hearts and open minds, trusting the Holy Mystery to guide us into a new order that will help us live into the future. Perhaps my fictional character Neo's guided tour of the past will help you see that real-world possibility more clearly. •

As noted in the second paragraph, the bulk of this article is an edited excerpt from Brian D. McLaren, A New Kind of Christian: A Tale of Two Friends on a Spiritual Journey (Minneapolis: Fortress, 2019), 41–56. All rights reserved.

Please Call Me by My True Names

1 Reprinted from pages 72–73 of *Call Me by My True Names: The Collected Poems of Thich Nhat Hanh* (1999) by Thich Nhat Hanh with permission of Parallax Press, Berkeley, California, www.parallax.org.

Include and Transcend

1 Walter Brueggemann, *Spirituality of the Psalms* (Minneapolis: Fortress, 2002), 9–11.

2 Daniel Breazeale, trans. and ed., *Fichte: Early Philosophical Writings* (Ithaca, NY: Cornell University Press, 1993), 63.

3 G. I. Gurdjieff, *Beelzebub's Tales to His Grandson* (New York: Penguin, 1950), 138.

4 Paul Ricœur, *The Symbolism of Evil* (Boston: Beacon, 1967), 351.

The Law of Three

1 James Moore, *Gurdjieff: The Anatomy of a Myth* (Rockport, MA: Element, 1991), 44.

2 Maurice Nicoll, *Psychological Commentaries on the Teaching of Ouspensky and Gurdjieff* (Boulder: Shambhala, 1984), 111–112.

3 P. D. Ouspensky, *In Search of the Miraculous: Fragments of an Unknown Teaching* (New York: Harcourt Brace Jovanovich, 1976), 78.

4 Jacob Needleman, *What Is God?* (New York: Jeremy P. Tarcher/Penguin, 1983), 96.

Emerging Wisdom Patterns in the Black Lives Matter Movement

1 "John Lewis' Last Words," *The Atlanta Journal-Constitution*, July 30, 2020, https://www.ajc.com/john-lewis/john-lewis-last-words/GGQ6MKJTIBHGHJ7RQXZVLQFHUA/.

2 The Pew Research Center examined tweets that included the phrase Black Lives Matter; Monica Anderson, "The Hashtag #BlackLivesMatter Emerges: Social Activism on Twitter," *Pew Research Center*, August 15, 2016, http:www.pewinternet.org/2016/08/15/the-hashtag-blacklivesmatter-emerges-social-activism-on-twitter.

3 Jelani Cobb, "The Matter of Black Lives: A New Kind of Movement Found Its Moment. What Will Its Future Be?" *The New Yorker*, March 14, 2016, https://www.newyorker.com/magazine/2016/03/14/where-is-black-lives-matter-headed.

4 Ibid. Mehserle was convicted of involuntary manslaughter and served one year of a two-year sentence. Alicia Garza, a founder of BLMM, lived only a few blocks away from the shooting.

5 Senator Mitch McConnell repeated the intent of his party in an interview that appeared in the *National Journal* on October 23, 2010; "Top GOP Priority: Make Obama a One-Term President," https://www.nationaljournal.com/member/magazine/top-gop-priority-make-obama-a-one-term-president-20101023/.

6 Cobb, "The Matter of Black Lives."

7 Ryan W. Miller, "Black Lives Matter: A Primer on What It Is and What It Stands For," *USA Today*, July 11, 2016, http://www.usatoday.com/story/news/nation/2016/07/11/black-lives-matter-what-what-stands/86963292/.

8 "SNCC, a Black legacy organization catalyzed by Ella Baker in 1960 and staffed by hundreds of Black organizers and volunteers, implemented a comprehensive field program to mobilize and engage young Black activists in the fight for freedom and liberation. From voter registration drives to Freedom Rides, SNCC paved the way for Black organizing and Black power." Black Lives Matter, "'Y'all Take It from Here': Delegates from the Student Nonviolent Coordinating Committee Champion the Movement for Black Lives," *Portside.org*, August 11, 2016, https://portside.org/2016-08-11/yall-take-it-here-delegates-student-nonviolent-coordinating-committee-champion-movement.

9 G. E. Bentley, ed., *William Blake: The Critical Heritage* (Abingdon-on-Thames, UK: Taylor & Francis, 2002), 30, note 1.

10 Michael Eric Dyson, *I May Not Get There with You: The True Martin Luther King, Jr.* (New York: Touchstone, 2001), chap. 10.

11 As quoted in Black Lives Matter, "'Y'all Take It from Here.'"

12 "John Lewis' Last Words."

13 Osagie K. Obasogie and Zachary Newman, "Black Lives Matter and Respectability Politics in Local News Accounts of Officer-Involved Civilian Deaths: An Early Empirical Assessment," *Wisconsin Law Review* 541, no. 3 (2016): Abstract.

14 Dietrich Bonhoeffer's famous quote, "We are not to simply bandage the wounds of victims beneath the wheels of injustice, we are to drive a spoke into the wheel itself," is taken from the essay "The Church and the Jewish Question," in Renate Wind, *Dietrich Bonhoeffer: A Spoke in the Wheel* (Grand Rapids: William B. Eerdmans, 2002), 69.

15 John Blake, "Is Black Lives Matter Blowing It?" *CNN*, August 2, 2016, http://www.cnn.com/2016/07/29/us/black-lives-matter-blowing-it/.

16 Rev. Osagyefo Sekou in Andrew Wilkes, "Living in the End Times: An Interview with Rev. Osagyefo Sekou," *ReligiousSocialism.org*, May 16, 2015, https://www.religioussocialism.org/_an_interview_with_rev_sekou.

17 Reinhold Niebuhr, *The Irony of American History* (Chicago: The University of Chicago Press, 1952), 63.

18 James Weldon Johnson, "Lift Every Voice and Sing," 1899.

19 Kendrick Lamar, "Alright," *To Pimp a Butterfly*, Top Dawg Entertainment, 2015.

Looking Back to Look Ahead

1 C. S. Lewis, *The Discarded Image: An Introduction to Medieval and Renaissance Literature* (Cambridge, UK: Cambridge University Press, 1964), 219–220.

2 Ibid., 98–100.

3 Ibid., 221.

4 Ibid., 222.

5 Ibid., 222–223.

Coming Spring 2021!

Trauma, Vol. 9, No. 1

IN HIS INTRODUCTION to the Spring 2021 edition of *Oneing*, Richard Rohr states that "there has scarcely been a protracted period, family, or country which did not regularly experience such things as war, famine, torture, a tragic loss of parents or children, unbearable injustice over which a group felt powerless, visible domestic violence, violent rape, false imprisonment, flood or fire on a massive scale, or even wholesale genocide of a race or village."

The theme of the edition is timely, considering the loss of hundreds of thousands of lives due to a complex global pandemic, political upheaval, armed conflicts, and squalid migrant camps cropping up in many parts of the world, not to mention the suffering of countless kinds of animal and plant life due to global warming. Although it seems that we are living through eschatological times, we can hope that transformation will be the result of this eye-opening, heartbreaking suffering.

To help us make sense of seemingly endless personal and collective traumas, the edition will feature fine authors from a variety of backgrounds, including the healing arts. New voices to *Oneing*, such as Trina Avetta Armstrong, Elizabeth Lev, and Mike Petrow will be featured alongside familiar, previously published names, including David Benner, Joan Halifax, James Finley, Matthew Fox, and Kaitlin Curtice.

Both the limited-print edition of CAC's literary journal,
Oneing, and the downloadable PDF version
will be available for sale in April 2021
at https://store.cac.org/.

Center for
Action and
Contemplation

A collision of opposites forms the cross of Christ.
One leads downward preferring the truth of the humble.
The other moves leftward against the grain.
But all are wrapped safely inside a hidden harmony:
One world, God's cosmos, a benevolent universe.